The Entrepreneur's Guide
Habit Hacks for Start-up Success

Judy E. Campbell

Table of Contents

1. Introduction 2
2. Setting the Stage: The Importance of Habits in Entrepreneurship 3
    2.1. Understanding Habits: The Invisible Architects of Success 3
    2.2. The Power of Keystone Habits: Creating a Domino Effect 4
    2.3. Habits in the Entrepreneurial Journey: Possible Pitfalls and Their Mitigation 5
3. Mastering Your Morning: Waking Up to Success 7
    3.1. The Power of Rising Early 7
    3.2. Developing a Morning Routine 8
    3.3. Nourishing Your Body 8
    3.4. Leveraging Mornings for Critical Thinking 9
    3.5. Conclusion 9
4. The Power of Routine: Structuring Your Entrepreneurial Day 11
    4.1. The Core Understanding of Routine 11
    4.2. The Building Blocks of a Fruitful Routine 12
    4.3. The Power of Rituals in Your Routine 12
    4.4. The Enriching Impact of Regular Exercise 13
    4.5. Holding onto Flexibility in Your Routine 13
5. Strategic Breaks: Relaxation for Enhanced Productivity 15
    5.1. Realizing the Power of Breaks 15
    5.2. Creating Your Break Matrix 16
    5.3. Relaxation Techniques for Optimum Revitalization 17
    5.4. The Shift Towards Quality Rest 18
6. Mind Nutrition: Information Consumption Habits 19
    6.1. The Infodiet: What Are You Consuming? 19
    6.2. Strategic Information Consumption: Why and How 20
    6.3. Saying No To Information Overload 20

- 6.4. The Power of Selective Ignorance ... 21
- 6.5. Enrichment Through Thought Leadership ... 21
- 7. Entrepreneurial Fitness: Physical Activity and Success ... 23
  - 7.1. The Dynamic Duo: Health and Productivity ... 23
  - 7.2. Let's Get Moving: Incorporating Physical Activity ... 24
  - 7.3. The Entrepreneur's Workout Regimen ... 25
- 8. Making Every Minute Count: Time Management Techniques ... 26
  - 8.1. Harnessing the Power of Prioritization ... 26
  - 8.2. Time Blocking: A Structured Approach to Productivity ... 27
  - 8.3. Efficiency Through Task Batching ... 27
  - 8.4. Mitigating Distractions: An Exercise of Discipline ... 28
  - 8.5. Evaluating Your Time: Taking Accountability ... 28
- 9. The Learning Curve: Habits for Continuous Improvement ... 30
  - 9.1. The Ayana of Continuous Improvement ... 30
  - 9.2. The Habit of Learning: A Critical Examination ... 31
  - 9.3. The Application of Knowledge ... 31
  - 9.4. Creating a Feedback Loop for Improvement ... 32
  - 9.5. Building Resilience: The Habit of Perseverance ... 32
- 10. Network Smarter: Leveraging Relationships in Business ... 34
  - 10.1. The Art of Networking ... 34
  - 10.2. Be a Valuable Listener ... 34
  - 10.3. Importance of Emotional Intelligence ... 35
  - 10.4. Role of Social Media ... 35
  - 10.5. Nurturing Relationships ... 35
  - 10.6. Networking Events & Conferences ... 36
  - 10.7. Leveraging Business Relationships ... 36
  - 10.8. Seek Mentorship ... 36
  - 10.9. Foster Collaboration ... 36
  - 10.10. Identifying Opportunities ... 37
- 11. Rolling with Punches: Resilience in Face of Challenges ... 38

11.1. The Essence of Resilience in Entrepreneurship 38
11.2. The Making of a Resilient Entrepreneur 39
11.3. Nurturing Resiliency - Practical Approaches 39
11.4. Resilience is the Key to Entrepreneurial Success 40

Entrepreneurship is living a few years of your life like most people won't, so that you can spend the rest of your life like most people can't.

— Warren G. Tracy

Chapter 1. Introduction

Delve into a world where success is not just a result of hard work, but also a meticulous cultivation of empowering habits. Welcome to "The Entrepreneur's Guide: Habit Hacks for Start-up Success." This enlightening Special Report is designed to illuminate your entrepreneurial path, busting through the myths of startup culture and replacing them with purposeful, productivity-boosting behaviors and routines. Far from textbook technical, this guide is all about demystifying the secrets of successful entrepreneurs and condensing them into actionable insights for you to leverage. With every flip of a page, may your dread of uncertainties be replaced by the thrill to conquer and your quest for entrepreneurial zenith gain an invincible pace. Get ready to transform your startup journey from stressful to successful - and all it takes is a little bit of habit hacking!

Chapter 2. Setting the Stage: The Importance of Habits in Entrepreneurship

What greets us at birth is a vast expanse of possibilities, and it takes years of conditioning and experiences to tap into, and expand upon, this raw potential that lies within us. The habits we form become a defining feature of our identities. They shape our lives, transforming the infinite potential of our minds into progressive actions and productive outcomes. The profound significance of habits is not restricted to individuals but extends to the realms of entrepreneurship as well. The entrepreneurial journey could very well be likened to a rudderless ship caught in a tumultuous storm, the outcome of which would depend largely on the Habitscape of the entrepreneur at the helm.

2.1. Understanding Habits: The Invisible Architects of Success

As entrepreneurs, the significance of our habits is often overshadowed by pressing issues of strategy, investment, and growth. These facets cannot be undermined; however, it is equally crucial to understand that beneath the complex mechanics of business, it is the habits that seethe unseen, influencing actions, decisions, and, ultimately, the trajectory of the startup's success.

The human brain, with its immense complexity, is perpetually seeking ways to conserve energy. Repeated actions, sayings, behaviors, or decisions are bundled and relegated to the automatic series of tasks by the brain – these we identify as habits. Once formed, they function without conscious engagement, often outside the bromides of right and wrong. It is thus of paramount importance to cultivate and operate on empowering habits that will assiduously fuel the entrepreneurial engine towards success.

Understanding and adopting these habit-stimulating strategies is pivotal. Studies consistently show that entrepreneurs who integrate productive habits into their daily life have a higher probability of building successful businesses. They're the invisible architects of success, holding the power to precipitate achievements and parlay raw ambition into effective operations.

2.2. The Power of Keystone Habits: Creating a Domino Effect

A prominent concept in the harnessing power of habits is the idea of keystone habits. These are habits that, once established, set off a cascade of other actions and routines that are conducive to overall success. They can vary greatly among individuals. For some entrepreneurs, a keystone habit can be as simple as maintaining a task planner, while for others, it might involve a rigorous workout regime or a dedicated meditation routine. The trick lies in identifying and nurturing such habits that can trigger a positive chain of actions.

Keystone habits create structures that can magnetize other good habits and replace the less productive ones. When our brain establishes a routine or a ritual, it lessens our dependence on willpower and decision-making capacities. With streamlined routines, each day can begin with triumph, creating a momentum that cascades throughout the day, pushing us towards our goals.

2.3. Habits in the Entrepreneurial Journey: Possible Pitfalls and Their Mitigation

However, with power comes responsibility, and with the rhythm derived from habits, comes the potential for establishing and fostering undesirable patterns. It's important to note that unwholesome habits, once ingrained, can lead to damaging consequences.

For instance, the habit of working late into the night, fueled by the fear of missing out on potential opportunities, can infringe on the much-needed sleep, relaxation, and rejuvenation time. It can spiral into increased stress levels, poor decision-making capabilities, and eventually, burnout. The mitigation lies in recognizing such pitfalls early on and approaching them with corrective measures. A deep awareness of your actions, patterns, and aids can facilitate kick-starting the process of change.

Remember, shifting habits is not an overnight process. It requires patience, commitment, and above all, understanding. Starting small, celebrating victories, 'stacking' habits, and creating implementation intentions are some science-backed strategies that can kickstart the process of change.

Believe in the power of change, of growth, and of your ability to shape your destiny through the habits you cultivate. As an entrepreneur, the world you create is not just a projection of your dreams, it is a mirror reflecting your habits. And it is in your hands to adjust that reflection by adjusting your habits. Your journey is unique, and so will be your habitscape. So, ponder, deliberate, and embark upon this journey of habit cultivation with an open mind and a willing heart.

Let us walk ahead into this transformative venture, for it is a journey worth undertaking. A journey towards building an empire where habits serve as the pillars of stability amid the storm that entrepreneurship invariably triggers. And it is these pillars that will ensure that your ship not only withstands the storm but charts its course towards unprecedented heights of success. Let us dive deeper into specific habits in further chapters and excavate the keys to the kingdom of entrepreneurial success.

Chapter 3. Mastering Your Morning: Waking Up to Success

The alarm clock rings, marking the start of a new day. For many, the first instinct is to hit the snooze button, desperately seeking a few more moments of sleep. However, for the ambitious entrepreneur, those first few hours of the day set the tone for everything that follows. They offer an opportunity to build a strong foundation for the day's ventures, to recharge both mind and body, and start the day with a kick of productive energy.

3.1. The Power of Rising Early

Successful entrepreneurs, from Elon Musk to Richard Branson, swear by the habit of rising early to tackle the day. More than merely being about work, the early morning offers a quiet, uninterrupted environment conducive to thinking, planning, and preparing oneself both mentally and physically. During this sacred time, one can ease into the day, free from the bombardment of emails, phone calls, and distractions that often accompany later hours. Furthermore, getting up early creates a sense of control over one's day, giving the feeling that they are ahead of the game.

Consider Benjamin Franklin's renowned saying, "Early to bed, early to rise, makes a man healthy, wealthy and wise." This simple adage underlines the potential benefits of making the most out of your mornings. By waking up early, you are providing your mind with a fresh canvas onto which you can paint the rest of your day, untainted by the stresses that often gather as the day progresses.

3.2. Developing a Morning Routine

A regular morning routine is a common thread among successful entrepreneurs. This routine acts as a form of conditioning, priming the mind, and body for the day ahead. Each routine will vary depending on the individual, as it should be personalized to one's needs and lifestyle. However, a few universal activities are worth considering.

First on the list is physical activity. Whether it be a brisk walk, a run, yoga, or a full-blown workout, any form of exercise aids in waking up the body, boosting energy levels, and forming a refreshingly revitalizing starting point for your day.

Next in line is meditation or mindfulness-related activities. Providing yourself with a quiet moment to clear your mind, sip a cup of calming tea, or practice some deep breathing exercises can do wonders for your mental health and focus. This period of tranquility can pave the way for a calm, collected demeanor throughout the day.

Following this, an entrepreneur can dive into planning their day using methods like the Eisenhower Decision Matrix to distinguish between urgent and important tasks and allocate time accordingly. By setting clear goals for the day, one can be well-prepared to tackle whatever comes their way.

Furthermore, building in some time for learning - like reading, watching educational videos, or listening to podcasts - can supplement your knowledge base and spark creativity. A perpetual investment in self-improvement is vital for an entrepreneur's start-up journey.

3.3. Nourishing Your Body

Breakfast is often proclaimed as the most important meal of the day, and with good reason. A nutritious breakfast fuels the body, replenishes the glucose levels necessary for brain function, and kickstarts metabolism. It's essential, therefore, to make time for a balanced breakfast instead of rushing out the door on an empty stomach.

Beyond the meal itself, remaining hydrated is pivotal. Start the day with a glass of water; it refreshes your system after the long hours of sleep and is linked with increased alertness.

3.4. Leveraging Mornings for Critical Thinking

The morning quiet can be used as a sanctuary for deep-work and critical thinking. When the world is still waking up, it's easier to engage in complex problem-solving or strategic planning with a refreshed mind free from distractions.

Regardless of how you choose to utilize this time, remember that successful entrepreneurship isn't simply about working longer hours. It's about maximizing productivity within the working hours and utilizing personal time for other essential aspects such as health, learning, and self-improvement.

3.5. Conclusion

Mastering your morning isn't about adhering to every step discussed above rigidly. It's about understanding the value these first few golden hours of the day bring and tailoring a routine that fits your lifestyle and work ethic. By combining the principles of early rising, physical and mental conditioning, strategic planning, a hearty breakfast, and critical thinking, you equip yourself with a blueprint for a productive, fulfilling day that feeds your entrepreneurial journey. After all, every morning presents itself as a new opportunity to ascend towards the success you're dreaming of. Be sure to seize it.

Chapter 4. The Power of Routine: Structuring Your Entrepreneurial Day

For countless aspiring entrepreneurs, there's a profound tendency to associate their approach to work with a disarrayed, chaotic schedule that orbits around the principle of working ceaselessly, often fondly referred to as 'hustling'. However, such a fray not only impedes your productivity but also trails to inevitable burnout. Our exploration to structuring your entrepreneurial day revolves around a mechanism that adheres to a routine. A method to combat that inefficacy, convoluted complications, and the draining of mental resources is the power of incorporating routine into your entrepreneurial day.

4.1. The Core Understanding of Routine

Routines serve as psychological constructs designed to streamline our tasks. They offer a series of neatly arranged actions into a reliable and comfortable pattern. This takes a handful of actions and transforms them into a chunk of automation, freeing up cognitive resources for higher-order thinking. A well-structured routine doesn't restrict; instead, it liberates, providing an empowering framework that eliminates the load of constant decision-making throughout your day.

Understanding what to do at any given time of the day draws away the turmoil of attending to an unforeseen sequence of tasks, consequently refining your focus and amplifying productivity. From the likes of Elon Musk to Tim Cook, renowned entrepreneurs mark their success trajectory with the brushstrokes of following a structured routine.

4.2. The Building Blocks of a Fruitful Routine

To initiate drafting your routine, it's instrumental to start by identifying your most productive hours, often termed as your 'prime time'. Studies have conveyed that people typically find their most focused and creative period in the mornings. In contrast, others might find the late-night serenity a prime time for their entrepreneurial exploits. Discovering your prime time is paramount to align the most demanding tasks to your highest energy levels.

Once you've recognized your prime time, assign it towards tackling the most significant tasks. The isolation of crucial tasks is a technique known as the 'Pareto Principle' or the 80/20 rule, which suggests that 80% of your outcomes will arise from 20% of your actions. By dedicating your prime time to these tasks, you effectively maximize usage of your peak energy and focus levels.

What follows is ensuring regular intervals of rest and disconnection. The human cognitive structure isn't designed for indefinite periods of focused, intensive work. Conscious breaks, often referred to as 'strategic breaks', are integral to enhance long-term productivity.

4.3. The Power of Rituals in Your Routine

Entrepreneurial routines are greatly amplified with the integration of specific rituals. These rituals, whether they are an invigorating stretch before commencing work, a warm cup of tea during breaks, or watching uplifting content post-work, inject a personalized element into your routine that aids in signifying transitions between different phases of the day. They help reinforce the routine, making it easier to slip into the pattern and reinforcing the positive responses related with completing tasks.

4.4. The Enriching Impact of Regular Exercise

Incorporation of physical exercise into your routine is often overlooked, especially by novice entrepreneurs inundated with an array of operational responsibilities. However, research has consistently shown that regular physical activity plays a pivotal role in enhancing cognitive abilities, boosting productivity, and mitigating stress levels. Be it a morning jog, midday yoga, or an evening walk, integrating an exercise regimen in your routine contributes towards physical fitness, superior concentration, and an overall improved mental well-being.

4.5. Holding onto Flexibility in Your Routine

While the essence of a routine lies in consistency, its application shouldn't tread the thin line of becoming rigid. The entrepreneurial journey is imbued with unanticipated circumstances and calls for adaptability. Therefore, although your routine should serve as strong guidelines for how you structure your day, it shouldn't be a force-fit that restricts you from making necessary adjustments. Retaining some flexibility in your routine helps you account for unforeseen circumstances and encourages an agile entrepreneurial mindset.

In conclusion, by architecting an effective routine, entrepreneurs profoundly augment their ability to tackle the demanding landscape of creating and running a new venture. With a combination of identifying prime time, harnessing the Pareto Principle, incorporating rest and rituals, encouraging regular exercise, and maintaining a certain degree of flexibility, entrepreneurs can craft a structured, adaptable routine. It is this routine that has the potential to serve as the secret ingredient towards fueling an entrepreneurial day with harvestable productivity and enduring success. So unleash the power of routine and tread confidently on your entrepreneurial journey.

Chapter 5. Strategic Breaks: Relaxation for Enhanced Productivity

Pace, pace, and pace - that's the general metaphor often associated with an entrepreneur's life. From brainstorming innovative ideas, hustling for resources, developing prototypes, to chasing potential customers. The relentless cycles make it seem like rest and relaxation are sentiments entrepreneurs cannot afford to encourage. However, this perspective might be leading most entrepreneurs toward a productivity paradox. In their quest for incessant hustle and grind, they might forget the elemental role relaxation can play in enhancing productivity. The undeniable reality is that though counterintuitive at first glance, strategic breaks can bolster productivity, creativity, and overall entrepreneurial performance. Hence, going against the mainstream grain, this chapter aims at empowering you with the understanding and strategies to harness the power of strategic breaks as a way to realise enhanced productivity.

5.1. Realizing the Power of Breaks

Successful entrepreneurs realize the importance of creating an optimal balance between work and rest. This involves strategically scheduling breaks to rejuvenate their mind, body, and soul. Studies reveal that working continuously for long periods can result in burnout, decreased productivity, and dampened creativity.

Contrarily, organizing your work with intermittent rest periods can help reduce fatigue, improve focus and concentration, and also drive innovation. The pioneering research of Professor K. Anders Ericsson underlines the importance of deliberate breaks in enhancing performance. His studies reveal that top performers – be it musicians, athletes, or chess players – never work for more than 90 minutes at a stretch. Every intense work period is followed by a deliberate break that allows them to process new information, incorporate learned skills, and replenish energy reserves.

For entrepreneurs, it means that working smarter, not harder may be the way forward. This implies that one should not measure their success in term of hours spent in office, but the milestones achieved. You become more efficient and productive when you incorporate breaks into your work schedule, allowing your brain to relax and recharge. The value of strategic relaxation thus becomes less about the time it 'takes away' from work and more about the enhanced productivity it 'brings to' the work.

5.2. Creating Your Break Matrix

The concept of strategic breaks necessitates that they must be carefully planned and oriented towards rejuvenating your mind and body. It's not simply about lying on the couch aimlessly scrolling through your social media feed – although, occasionally, that might be exactly what you need.

Instead, it's about incorporating activities that relax your overworked brain and refresh your energy levels. You can craft a Break Matrix - a structured schedule highlighting different types of strategic breaks that complement your work and lifestyle.

The Break Matrix generally includes three types of breaks:

1. Micro-breaks: Frequent and short, lasting for 5-10 minutes after every 25-30 minutes of work. They can include simple activities like stretching, looking away from digital screens, or taking a quick walk to unwind and reset.

2. Mes0-breaks: Medium-duration breaks that last for about 15-20 minutes, planned after 90-120 minutes of work. They can involve leisurely activities that prompt mild exercise or passive cognitive

engagement, like walking, meditating, or reading a non-work related book.

3. Macro-breaks: Longer breaks, set aside for meals, exercise, or relaxation activities like hobbies or time with loved ones; ideally, spanning an hour or two.

The sweetness in this pie comes from the customizability. Since one's lifestyle, personality and preferences significantly vary, the Break Matrix can be personalized to suit each entrepreneur's unique needs and capabilities. The idea is not to uniformly follow the breaks, but to imbibe a habit of taking strategic pauses as required.

5.3. Relaxation Techniques for Optimum Revitalization

Strategic breaks provide you with an opportunity to relax and re-energize. But how you utilize these breaks makes all the difference. Here are some relaxation techniques known for their productivity-boosting powers:

- Meditation: It improves concentration, boosts creativity and helps alleviate stress. Just a few minutes of mindful breathing can help you return to work with renewed clarity and focus.
- Physical Exercise: Whether it's high-intensity workout or low-intensity yoga, physical activity stimulates our brain to release endorphins – the body's natural mood boosters.
- Hobbies: Engaging in activities that you love lets your brain relax while still maintaining a steady flow of dopamine, keeping your mood elevated and energy levels high.
- Naps: A short power nap of 20-30 minutes can help to improve mood, alertness, and performance. They are nature's way of recharging your brain, ensuring you return to work refreshed and revitalized.

That being said, not every relaxation technique may fit your work style or rhythm. It's essential to experiment with different techniques and choose those that work best for you.

5.4. The Shift Towards Quality Rest

Building on the misconception that entrepreneurs should always be working is not just counterproductive, it's unhealthy. With stress, burnout, and exhaustion being significant issues affecting entrepreneurs, the onus falls on you to prioritize your wellbeing. Realizing the criticality of strategic breaks and quality relaxation can contribute considerably to preventing potential productivity pitfalls.

In essence, what strategic breaks offer you is a more sustainable, healthy, and productive mode of operating. They ensure you don't just survive the entrepreneurial journey, but also enjoy and thrive through it. So, shed the stale norms, embrace the power of relaxation, and experience a noticeable enhancement in your vitality, creativity, productivity, and overall entrepreneurial success!

Chapter 6. Mind Nutrition: Information Consumption Habits

In the technological age we currently reside in, a most significant, yet often overlooked facet of our daily routines lies nestled within the information we routinely engage with. The assimilation of information, whether through active targeting or passive scrolling, has the power to mold us into both dynamic problem solvers and initiative-taking game changers within the business circuit. The more pertinent issue, however, is the quality and relevance of the information that enters our minds. It is akin to the old saying - 'You are what you eat,' yet in this context, we prefer to state - 'You are what you consume informationally.'

6.1. The Infodiet: What Are You Consuming?

Many would toy with the idea of an information diet, trouble in conceptualizing that the intellectual nutrients your brain needs parallel closely with your body's need for a balanced diet. Curating a healthy information diet involves careful incorporation of various forms of data, newsfeeds, studies, and narratives that could prove enriching to one's knowledge arsenal. However, it is equally crucial to eliminate or minimize exposure to information sources that tend to generate an overload, causing more harm than benefit.

Being selective in one's information intake demands technological savvy and self-awareness. Permit yourself those Instagram-scroll moments, but add balance by dedicating inevitable screen time to enlightening TED Talks, engage with thoughtfully penned business blogs, or embrace the wisdom dripping in well-curated podcasts. Aim for balance, seek out a variety of informational sources, and lean towards depth of understanding over sheer volume of knowledge.

6.2. Strategic Information Consumption: Why and How

Strategic information consumption has everything to do with intentionality, anchored firmly in the business goals you commendably pursue. Seek out content that aligns with your niche market, with the demographics and psychographics of your audience, with the cultural factors influencing your business environment. Embrace information that fosters growth, stimulates innovative thought, empowers decision making and further provides a compelling lens to survey the competitive landscape.

Strategic information consumers possess a goal-oriented framework for each engagement with text, audio, or video content. They understand the strength in investing time wisely on platforms that offer the enriched, detailed insights, urging you towards comprehensive reading, critical listening, and open-minded viewing.

6.3. Saying No To Information Overload

In the bustling internet age, the mammoth task before us is not finding information, but sifting through it purposefully. Information overload is a real danger, swaying us off our focus path and leaving us in a state of confusion more often than not. As with everything else in life, moderation is key.

Structure your information diet to be nourishing rather than overwhelming. Allocate specific time-slots during your day for informational ingestion. Use tools and apps to streamline your reading. Feed readers like Feedly, organized principles like 'Inbox

Zero' for your email, or even the 'save' or 'read later' feature on social media platforms can act as digital allies in managing information.

6.4. The Power of Selective Ignorance

Selective ignorance is by no means a promotion of blissful ignorance, rather it encourages an awareness of how one's time and energy get distributed while consuming information. The idea is to prevent irrelevant, redundant, or distracting information from occupying precious cognitive real estate. This notion finds roots in the Pareto Principle - 20% of the information will yield 80% of needed insights. Henceforth, it is not always necessary to have your head buried in data. Adopt the ability to discern what information fuels your entrepreneurial motivation and what merely adds to unnecessary cognitive load.

6.5. Enrichment Through Thought Leadership

While incorporating diversified sources and establishing effective strategies towards information consumption, it is equally critical to cultivate the habit of enrichment through thought leadership. This involves not just passive consumption, but engaging in active dialogue, creating and sharing content. Forming thought leadership habits strengthens your brand identity, extends your network, and places you in the trajectory of career advancement.

Facing the surges and ebbs of the informational tide is part and parcel of an entrepreneur's journey. The ability to deliberately and mindfully engage with this vast ocean of knowledge can undoubtedly color the horizon of entrepreneurial success. By forging your information consumption habits, you'll soon find that the navigation towards your envisioned success becomes a lot more deliberate, a lot more attainable, and a multitude more enjoyable.

Chapter 7. Entrepreneurial Fitness: Physical Activity and Success

It goes without saying that the journey of entrepreneurship is both mentally and emotionally challenging. As we delve deeper into our enterprise, we often find ourselves entrapped in a vicious cycle, where we are consistently pushing our boundaries, neglecting the fundamental cornerstone of all our endeavors - our health. However, an astute entrepreneur comprehends the significance of harmonizing their cognitive prowess with physical strength. The adage, "a healthy mind resides in a healthy body," holds much truth for the entrepreneur who seeks to excel. Preserving and enhancing our health, therefore, becomes not just a need, but an entrepreneurial success strategy.

7.1. The Dynamic Duo: Health and Productivity

Imagine running a marathon without training for it. Surely, you would feel overwhelmingly stressed and exhausted - a state that may not be far from what an entrepreneur experiences while navigating the startup labyrinth. They are met with an unceasing barrage of stressors that demand their utmost mental resilience. However, the mind's ability to ward off stress, generate ingenious solutions, and maintain an unwavering focus is inherently limited by the body's health. Thus, physical fitness isn't merely a lifestyle choice, but a strategic necessity for the thriving entrepreneur.

A wealth of scientific research supports the correlation between physical activity and brain health. Regular physical activity enhances cognitive function due to increased blood flow, and better oxygen and nutrient delivery to the brain. It results in improved concentration, memory, creativity, and problem-solving ability - the very weapons in an entrepreneur's arsenal. Impressively, physical exercise has been found to stimulate neurogenesis - the production of new neurons, a process pivotal to cognitive flexibility and learning capacity.

Moreover, the hormones released during exercise, especially endorphins, often referred to as 'feel-good' hormones, help to combat stress, anxiety, and depression, fostering a positive mindset. Sleep, another fundamental pillar of mental health and cognitive function, is vastly improved with regular physical activity. As every entrepreneur knows, burnout is a formidable foe to productivity. Good physical health equips you with the fortitude to resist burnout, enhancing your business performance.

7.2. Let's Get Moving: Incorporating Physical Activity

Now that we understand why physical fitness is crucial for entrepreneurship, the question is, how do we incorporate it into our packed schedule? Making time for physical activity is challenging but more than achievable. It just requires proactive planning and commitment.

Firstly, schedule your physical activity as you do your business meetings. Don't let it be an afterthought, something you'd do if, and when, you find time. It should be part of your daily routine. Whether you choose to work out early in the morning to jumpstart your day or in the evening to unwind effectively, consistency is key.

Mix up your routine to prevent boredom. Try different types of exercises such as cardio for heart health, resistance training for muscle and bone strength, and yoga or tai-chi for flexibility and mental peace. Ideally, aim for at least 150 minutes of moderate aerobic activity or 75 minutes of vigorous activity a week, along with strength training exercises twice a week.

7.3. The Entrepreneur's Workout Regimen

Working out doesn't necessarily mean spending hours at the gym; it can be adapted to your preferences and schedule. Here are few workouts techniques tailored for entrepreneurs:

1. High-Intensity Interval Training (HIIT): This involves short bursts of intensively strenuous activities interspersed with recovery periods. It's an effective and time-efficient way to exercise.
2. Deskercises: These are exercises that can be done right at your desk, such as chair squats, desk push-ups, seated leg raises among others.
3. Walking Meetings: Instead of traditional sitdown meetings, try active meetings like walk and talks. It improves creativity, mood, and collaboration.
4. Exercise Snacking: It refers to brief bouts of exercise that fit into everyday life, like taking stairs, parking far away from your destination to walk, or even dancing to a favorite song.

Remember, fitness isn't only about looking good; it's about well-being and staying sharp to tackle the entrepreneurial storm. As the entrepreneur's journey unfolds, ensuring physical fitness is not merely a desirable add-on but an indispensable element of the success blueprint. After all, success comes to those who not only dream big but also who take care of the vessel—mind and body—that transforms dreams into reality. Let the quest for entrepreneurial success and physical fitness ride harmoniously alongside each other, fueling your journey towards the summit of your aspiration.

Chapter 8. Making Every Minute Count: Time Management Techniques

In the entrepreneurial world, time is indeed gold; it is a precious, non-renewable resource, and once wasted, can never be restored. Generating maximum value requires mastery in crafting and controlling our minutes and hours, culminating in purpose-driven days, singularly focused on entrepreneurial success. This crucial chapter of our journey dives deep into the mechanisms of sound time management, providing you with a virtual toolbox filled to the brim with actionable techniques and methods.

8.1. Harnessing the Power of Prioritization

The baseline of any effective time management strategy is essentially prioritizing tasks. This entails having a clear understanding of which tasks carry the biggest weight concerning your business' objectives. Successful entrepreneurs don't just work hard, but they also work smart. They recognize that not all tasks are created equal, some having a wider impact on the company's growth trajectory.

One popular prioritization method is the Eisenhower Box or Matrix, coined from the practices of former U.S. President Dwight Eisenhower. He broke tasks down into four quadrants based on their urgency and significance: Important and Urgent, Important but not Urgent, Not Important but Urgent, and Not Important and Not Urgent.

Practicing this technique instills an improved method of addressing tasks depending on their value. It discourages 'fire-fighting', the tendency to always react to urgent matters, and instead promotes a conscious effort to focus on tasks of great importance – those contributing towards long-term goals.

8.2. Time Blocking: A Structured Approach to Productivity

Another cornerstone technique for time efficiency is time blocking. This involves dedicating specific time slots in your day for individual tasks or clusters of similar tasks. By defining the start and end time of activity blocks, cueing into our brains that there is a finite time to complete a job, we bolster our focus and productivity.

Successful time blocking encompasses both 'maker' and 'manager' timeframes. Maker periods are devoted to deep work, allowing for an undisturbed, productive flow. The manager hours, on the other hand, are meant for meetings, handling emails, and attending to administrative errands, thereby preventing disruption of focused maker blocks.

8.3. Efficiency Through Task Batching

Task batching is a fitting complement to time blocking—a workflow strategy that groups complementary tasks together to minimize constant brain switching. This technique is anchored in understanding the Pomodoro Technique's conception of a phenomenon called 'attention residue,' where the mind retains remnants of the previously performed tasks as one shuttles between different activities.

By batching analogous tasks, such as responding to emails or managing social media accounts, we prune out the time lost in counter-productive context-switching. Task batching might seem counterintuitive when faced with a multitude of diverse tasks, but its proficiency is rooted in the heightened focus and reduced cognitive dissonance it offers.

8.4. Mitigating Distractions: An Exercise of Discipline

The battle against time loss wouldn't be complete without addressing one of the biggest hindrances to productivity: distractions. Digital intruders such as social media notifications, non-urgent emails, and incessant messaging can fracture your focus and lead to a significant time sink.

Strategies to mitigate distractions include turning off non-essential app notifications, designating specific time for digital activities, and maintaining a tidy, distraction-free workspace. Understanding the insidious nature and impact of these distractions can empower entrepreneurs to regain control over their time.

8.5. Evaluating Your Time: Taking Accountability

Taking stock of how you spend your time is an eye-opening exercise in accountability. Tools like time-audit apps can provide granular data about where your hours and minutes go, unveiling time leaks and helping optimize use. This element of a successful time management routine intimates that inspection is as important as implementation.

Positively manipulating and controlling your time comes with the domain of entrepreneurship. It is an ongoing experiment that needs continuous improvement, feedback, and adjustments. The techniques provided herewith—the powerful act of prioritizing, the structured approach of time blocking, the efficiency optimization presented by task batching, the discipline demanded in distraction mitigation, and the accountability asked for in time evaluation—these are revered temporal navigation tools on the path to startup triumph.

Undoubtedly, time management is an important gear in the complex machinery of entrepreneurism. As we delve deeper into other entrepreneurial habits, remember that the ability to make every minute count lies within the power of your hands. You have the opportunity to dictate the narrative of your entrepreneurial journey. Rather than being overwhelmed by the tide of responsibilities, make the time your ally. The principle, "Time is money," has long instilled its echo in business corridors, and mastering its truth equips you with an inimitable edge in your entrepreneurial odyssey.

Chapter 9. The Learning Curve: Habits for Continuous Improvement

The ability to continuously improve and learn is a cornerstone of entrepreneurship, often shifting the scales in favor of those who embrace it. A consuming flame does not differentiate between esteemed woods and humble straws – it consumes both vigorously. Likewise, the entrepreneurial arena does not spare the complacent, irrespective of their laurels. Therefore, as you march forward on your journey, it is crucial to evolve continually, adapting and growing in sync with the changing dynamics.

9.1. The Ayana of Continuous Improvement

Continuous improvement, a concept deeply embedded in Japanese culture, is described by the term 'Kaizen.' Kaizen, which translates literally to 'good change,' is a no-nonsense approach to personal and business improvement alike. It requires the commitment to making small, incremental improvements regularly, resulting in substantial changes over time. The Kaizen methodology, though initially conceptualized for post-war industrial Japan, fits perfectly within our context.

Embracing the Kaizen philosophy involves focusing on improvement areas, deciding on achievable goals, implementing changes, and reviewing outcomes. This loop continues unabated, with each cycle adding another layer to your entrepreneurial prowess. Accepting this approach is akin to boarding a perpetual train of growth.

9.2. The Habit of Learning: A Critical Examination

Once you have adopted the Kaizen methodology, it's time to dissect the actual process of learning. Learning, often dismissed as a simple process of acquiring knowledge, is a multifaceted phenomenon, demanding exertion from various cognitive domains. It involves knowledge absorption, comprehension, application, and memory reinforcement. Each of these cognitive functions consumes energy, and therefore, their time management becomes imperative.

To manage this, entrepreneurs must cultivate a disciplined approach to learning new skills. This can involve dedicated learning hours, structured courses, or peer learning groups. The goal is to approach learning systematically, rather than sporadically. Each organized effort invested in learning moves you closer to your entrepreneurial peak.

9.3. The Application of Knowledge

Knowing is not enough. The quintessential habit of successful entrepreneurs is their ability to apply knowledge optimally and creatively in real-life scenarios. It's not about how many books you've read or seminars you've attended, but how the knowledge gained from these sources has been extrapolated to your business context, leading to value addition and problem-solving.

To inculcate this habit, it is beneficial to practice contextual learning. For instance, if you are learning about strategic planning, try to devise a strategic plan for a hypothetical, or your real business situation. In this way, you learn the concepts and simultaneously hone your ability to apply them. This duality fortifies your learning experience, providing an unshakeable foundation to expand on.

9.4. Creating a Feedback Loop for Improvement

There is no learning without feedback. Feedback underlines the shortcomings, progress, and potential improvement areas. Thus, developing a feedback system is indispensable. However, obtaining feedback can often be a challenge in the entrepreneurial landscape where you may be the top decision-maker. In such cases, seek external help. Business mentors, industry peers, even customers can provide valuable feedback that may reveal insights that were previously not on your radar.

Creating a feedback loop involves consistently seeking feedback, understanding it, making necessary adjustments, and learning from the entire process. Remember that feedback, positive or negative, is a vehicle for learning and improvement. Never shy away from it.

9.5. Building Resilience: The Habit of Perseverance

The entrepreneurial journey is marred by failures and setbacks. However, the habit of perseverance makes an entrepreneur resilient. It is critical to understand that failures are just learning opportunities in disguise. Developing a positive mindset towards failures and a determination to bounce back is the mark of a successful entrepreneur.

Cultivating the habit of perseverance also means developing endurance over time. This requires strategizing your daily tasks, managing your energy, and treating your health with the priority it deserves, all leading to a more resilient you.

Wrapping up, the process of continuous learning and improvement is a journey, not a destination. Embracing the Kaizen philosophy, adapting a structured approach to learning, applying knowledge, seeking feedback relentlessly, and cultivating the habit of perseverance are the vital ground rules to excel in this journey. Master these, and your entrepreneurial journey will transform from a struggling scramble to a confident stride, closer to your envisioned success summit with each step.

Chapter 10. Network Smarter: Leveraging Relationships in Business

In the grand symphony of entrepreneurship, relationships are the fingers that caress the right keys. They help to bring together an outburst of opportunities, ideas, and resources. Right from the moment of envisioning your start-up to the point of scaling up to the behemoth you aspire to be, your relationships will play an integral part. Let's explore how.

10.1. The Art of Networking

Networking is more of an art than a technique. It begins with understanding that you are the average of five people you spend most of your time with. Whether you are at a networking event, business conference, or even a coffee shop, being able to strike up meaningful conversations with people from various walks of life can be incredibly enriching. An important rule of networking, or the art of building influential relationships, is to impart value before expecting anything in return. When people perceive you as a valuable companion, they are more likely to reciprocate and help foster your professional growth.

10.2. Be a Valuable Listener

Sound interpersonal communication forms the backbone of networking. This primarily involves being a good listener. Entrepreneurs who genuinely listen to others' ideas and perspectives are better positioned to build strategic relationships. Actively listening also allows you to retain crucial information. This empowers you to formulate insightful responses, foster deeper connections, and engender potential collaborations.

10.3. Importance of Emotional Intelligence

Emotional intelligence is the unseen linchpin for networking success. The ability to empathize, express, and manage your feelings, as well as understand and influence the emotions of others, enables you to establish stronger connections. Higher emotional intelligence correlates with building deeper, more meaningful relationships, which in turn lead to business profitability and personal growth.

10.4. Role of Social Media

In this digital era, social media platforms are a powerful networking tool. They allow you to connect with like-minded individuals, potential clients, and industry influencers worldwide. Active participation in online communities relevant to your industry can help you gain visibility, credibility, and, eventually, facilitate valuable connections. Ensure you have a robust presence on key platforms and use them judiciously to enhance your networking strategy.

10.5. Nurturing Relationships

Like any growing entity, relationships need nurturing and care. Developing, maintaining, and enhancing relationships with professional associations serve as a vital infrastructure. This could involve simple gestures such as keeping in touch regularly, celebrating successes together, or offering help where you can. Remember that the strong relationships you cultivate today could transform into invaluable collaborations tomorrow.

10.6. Networking Events & Conferences

Networking events and conferences provide the perfect platform to meet a diverse array of people within your industry. Attending these events introduces you to new business trends, advice from seasoned professionals, and potential collaborations. Conferences and events provide a space for intentional networking, where entrepreneurs can continue cultivating their network and establishing new connections.

10.7. Leveraging Business Relationships

A crucial aspect of networking is the strategic deployment of your acquired relationships. Once you have established a network of mutual trust and respect, it is equally important to understand how to utilize these relationships for your entrepreneurial journey. This might involve seeking advice, sharing opportunities, or collaborating on projects.

10.8. Seek Mentorship

A strong network often introduces you to potential mentors who can offer crucial advice and guidance based upon their personal experiences. Reaching out to people within your network for mentorship not only helps you gain invaluable insights but also strengthens your bond with these individuals, fostering mutual growth.

10.9. Foster Collaboration

Successful entrepreneurs understand the power of collaboration.

Leverage your network to identify potential collaborations. This could be for a specific project, a business venture, or even knowledge exchange. Collaborations often lead to synergistic outcomes, where the combined effort yields greater results.

10.10. Identifying Opportunities

Your network can often be a source of opportunities, whether it is a new business avenue, a client lead, or a potential investor. Maintaining regular touchpoints with your contacts helps keep you in the loop for any opportunities that might arise.

In conclusion, networking is an essential skill that can significantly bolster your entrepreneurial journey. By mastering the art of networking, leveraging social media, nurturing relationships, and using these relationships strategically, you set yourself up for enduring success. From unlocking unexplored opportunities to building a reliable support system, strategic networking can be your secret weapon in the entrepreneurial battleground.

Chapter 11. Rolling with Punches: Resilience in Face of Challenges

Long winding pathways are not unknown in the world of entrepreneurship, as they are often engrossed with formidable challenges and daunting adversities. In this chapter, we will be decoding the intricate concept of resilience in the face of challenges and how that can unfold the prospect of greater success for entrepreneurs.

11.1. The Essence of Resilience in Entrepreneurship

Entrepreneurship is often likened to a rugged journey, brimming with unknown terrains and unexpected obstacles. Contrary to the hunky-dory image that most glorified narratives project, the path equally entails grueling hardships and trying times. These are the moments that truly test an entrepreneur's mettle, their tenacity, and the strength of their conviction. This where the concept of resilience threads into the entrepreneurial narrative, stitching up the loose ends, and bolstering the spirit of the entrepreneur.

Resilience in entrepreneurship is about the undying spirit to bounce back from setbacks, to learn from failures, and to not let the fear of stumbling deter from the pursuit of entrepreneurial goals. It's about treating every downturn as a learning curve, each setback as an opportunity to improve and advance.

11.2. The Making of a Resilient Entrepreneur

While resilience might appear to be an inherent quality to some, it is essentially a learned behavior, a product of experiences and the interpretations of these experiences. Among the multiple ways of nurturing entrepreneurial resilience, one of the most effective ones is fostering a growth mindset. Yes, a growth mindset - the one that perceives hurdles not as daunting dead ends, but mere detours leading to greater advancements.

Furthermore, resilient entrepreneurs tend to maintain a pragmatic understanding of the situation. They neither underestimate nor overinflate the gravity of the situation. They practice greater emotional intelligence, ensuring their cognitive faculties are not clouded by overwhelming emotions. This calls for a balanced act of emotional regulation and expression, which significantly enhances an entrepreneur's capability to navigate through challenging times.

11.3. Nurturing Resiliency - Practical Approaches

For those wondering how to percolate resilience into their entrepreneurial practice, here are some approaches you can consider.

1. Concentrate on Building Emotional Intelligence: Emotional intelligence refers to the ability to perceive, assess, and manage one's own and others' emotions. By developing this ability, entrepreneurs can better navigate through tough situations, interpret setbacks productively and maintain a balanced emotional state.

2. Develop a Growth Mindset: This involves seeing each challenge

as a springboard for growth and development rather than a blockade. Each setback is considered as an opportunity for learning and progression. For developing a growth mindset, focus on learning objectives over performance objectives.

3. Practice Mindfulness: Resilient entrepreneurs tend to incorporate mindfulness into their routine. Mindfulness allows entrepreneurs to remain present and fully engaged in the current scenario without getting overly reactive or overwhelmed.

4. Physical Well-being: The mind and the body share a symbiotic relationship. Mental resilience often has its roots in physical well-being. Incorporating regular exercise and mindful eating habits in the daily routine are steps in the right direction.

11.4. Resilience is the Key to Entrepreneurial Success

As we tread into the realm of entrepreneurship, it becomes increasingly clear that the journey is fraught with adversities and uncertainties. However, it is through these trials and tribulations that entrepreneurs learn the art of resilience. Forged in the fire of challenges, they utilize the power of resilience to push through the storm, keeping their entrepreneurial vision intact.

In conclusion, resilience is not just a survival mechanism, it's the entrepreneurial superpower that can turn around any daunting challenge into a stepping stone for success. And in this ever-evolving entrepreneurial landscape, it is the ones armed with resilience who stand a better chance to succeed. Cultivate this habit, brave the storm, and witness the phenomenal growth as an entrepreneur. Embarking on this journey might be overwhelming, but rest assured, you are now well-equipped with the know-how to form this empowering habit. Let resilience be your staunch ally, guiding you through the entrepreneurship journey with unwavering resolve and unprecedented success.

www.ingramcontent.com/pod-product-compliance
Lightning Source LLC
Chambersburg PA
CBHW070951220526
45471CB00007B/2985